Deion Thompson Armstrong

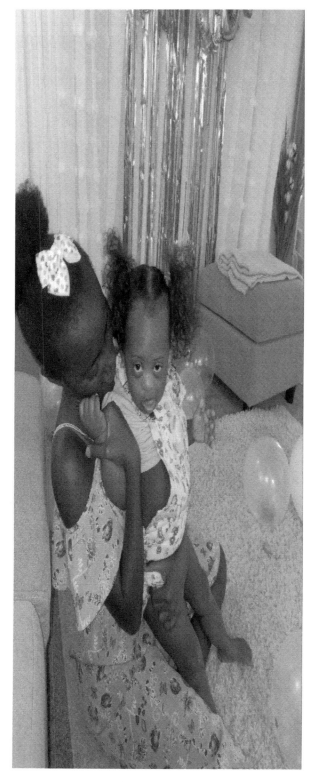

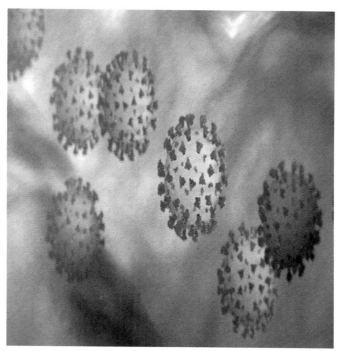

Chapter 1 Mr. Covid19
Fort Pierce- Sun going down, busy streets, malls and shopping centers

regenerating hope life sprung up so fast we ended the month of May 2020. It was dry, hot, and humid. Sometimes my body feels unable to breathe the cool and refreshing air that god provided for us. This lockdown made me panic. The grass was weathering, losing vibrant color, texture looking just as dead, it seemed like even the earth lost hope gosh. I prayed for rain and healing for our land, people and also for our nation's. Everything's dying. Children become scared, everyone feels that their loved ones won't be able to spend summer time ever again with each other. June arrived the rain poured nonstop, spring break their banks, a stream of heavy waters flooding the streets, weather alerts of thunderstorms watch, warnings were in effect for all other surrounding areas and various communities. Standing by the window I can see the birds flying away to the south, wow thank god our prayers have answered the rain fall and cooled our city down. Life was a bit hectic for me with not owning a car. I had to catch the bus to work. It was 5:15pm, the incumbent weather continued, I got out of my apartment and walked through the rushing water. It was three inches high, and my pants foot was soaking wet.My shoes weren't really wet as I wore hard high top timberland black in color. A few weeks earlier I forgot my umbrella on the number 1 bus during a changeover at Rio Mario Drive bus stop. I pulled my hoodie on my head, and a big white plastic bag over it to prevent my hair from getting wet.

Chapter 2 Panic

Lord have mercy but I was grateful for the many showers, lightning flashing,

the clapping of heavy thunder rolling, just frightening. This continue for 3 more days, on and off small raindrops drizzling in between, surprisingly the trees look greener, life has restored to the great cactus plant and the young palm trees that we fighting to survive, the birds chattering in the inhabitants returning to the sunshine city flying high in groups I look up in the sky wondering if they were having a party all kinds of different birds with such amazing color the environment sparkles you could tell that they were happy again. They had a lovely pond day swimming and flapping their wings. The baby duckling was diving too, laughing to myself just imagining how excited they were. I could see the Falcon strolling slowly on the streets, bee enjoying the lovely dainty Spanish needle, oh what a tremendous difference it makes when god intercede in our life. How wonderful and gracious are you, Lord? I prayed for the sick, helpless, and for those people that are in a state of becoming homeless, no jobs, crimes on the rise, loathing, shooting, and lots of demonstrations. The state's fear began to plague in my mind, the worst disease that I have ever encountered, anything like Mr. Covid19. Startled everyone he had killed our dreams, setting back growth, and development, no vaccine to control this deadly, dreadful pandemic, lots of life lost during the unrest. Systematically, its rapid testing shows scores of increases where lots of persons around the world have been tested positive, with all this happening more loss of life, people stop showing up for work every day. My job as an nursing assistant has become even more challenging we as staff member in the nursing industry face uncertainty each day of our live, we have to face the residents not knowing how to explaining why their family can't visit them anymore in my mind my heart was crumbling, asking myself how long will I continue to face this dilemma of the dangerous killer Covid19.

Chapter 3 Isolated

It is like an alien invasion on our planet, can you imagine how terrifying this is for us. Our temperature was recorded at the beginning of every shift throughout the entire workplace. We were tested Every 14 days, this became our new routine. Everyone wonders how long this will continue, spontaneously, we put our heart and soul to work protecting and safeguarding ourselves from this cruel monster. Social distance was the cure, it impacted the way that we function period. Hand washing is more frequent than ever, it was an awkward feeling ,but with Christ everything was possible, we live by the bible scripture fear not for I am with you, life changes suddenly virtual schooling , home schooling, graduation ceremony, everything that we could think of was now held online in a similar fashion "but god promises are true he said in his word if my people who called by my name will humble themselves and prayed and seek my face turned from their wicked way then I will hear from heaven and I will forgive them and will heal our land"(2 Chronicles 7 vs 14). Human beings felt that these words aren't powerful. Most of them become embarrassed, humiliated, and ashamed to acknowledge the bible and the words that are written to guide us as Christians, fasting and prayers is the key to fighting to make it through the storm. I never lose my way just like the testing of Daniel in the lion den I humble myself using coping skills, fasting was a tremendous tool that keep me from giving up, I look at how the greatest men in the olden days use this method not to fear but though doctrine, and scriptures, multiple souls were saved, people like job look to God for his healing, when he was cover in leprosy he believe in the word knowing that one day he was going to be cured from this weird disease, this awakening is one that will transform all of our life's in a very peculiar way.

Chapter 4 Route 1

One of the major steps is to pray constantly. Seeking God's presence in the midst of this pandemic just reminded men on earth that we should prepare to break up our way of life, and seek the lord, until he comes and reigns with us. Righteously, Jesus died on the cross for our sins yet people still fail to honor his commandment questioning the power of God seeking answers why Mr. Covid19 why? Because of the bad way we have our savior is showing us that he is still in control of our life. We go to church, we pray, but out of ignorance, jealousy, greed for wealth, we forget about our lord and savior Jesus Christ our soon coming king. Jesus teaches in the Bible that treasure awaits us in heaven. We are rich in the Lord so let's bow and worship him. Obeying the word of our father who art in heaven is a guide that builds our morality. I continue to pray to God in silence. Today I encourage the universe to trod by faith and not by sight. Wednesday misty weather lingers around, dark clouds appear, thick smoke moving swiftly in the air, darkness all around without any sign of the sun, there must be rain ahead. Baby cats racing each other across the old train track even the animals live under god instruction he created even the biggest   lions, that roar louder than a thunder but yet he can calm them I remember the story of Abraham and his son in those days God punished anyone who fail to obey   his word Abraham asked God, if he would destroy the earth because of 5 persons and the lord said I will not destroy the land because Abraham listening to the voice of his master think about the privilege men can get on this earth if we act in accordance with the spiritual begin who love us that he die for our sins, he was prosecuted, bruise for our transgression what a wonderful person. Delight yourself in the Lord o ye gates and be lifted up amongst all men Jesus will save more than ten thousand people by just coming as you are, the door of heaven is open to receive the saint and those who believe in his word shall be save as much as I know that we are the salt of the earth.

Chapter 5 The Family

We need to take into account that God will save our communities, cities, and nationwide through the admiration of prayers and fasting. We hoped that some Christian living in the moment knew that most of us refused to take up the cross and follow him salvation is free. The lord will forgive us of your sins if you seek him. Death without Christ is not valuable because there is no repentance in the grave, forget about diamonds, pearls, Bitcoin and other earthly values. In the end they have no true value, material things can't save us from sickness or death. generation cursed, causing a lot of people to be suffering from this weird unknown disease which attacks our lives. We have invisible barriers that block our new transgression. We must believe in change and understand that God is love, and he is the light of the world. I came to recognize that there is no one like you lord, nobody greater than you. We form a pray service at work each Tuesday it grows bigger, and better persons realizing that they all need Jesus in this trial time, a time that is full of pain, hurt, so many love one has passed away in a short time within a week and a half in my department Memory Care residents are dying slowly and alone to Mr. Covid19, this is a crucial pandemic, moving rapidly not wasting anytime. Residents getting frustrated not being able to see family members due to isolation were drained, miserable, and more confused. We realized some of them stop eating, refusing medications, and becoming traumatized, reluctantly only some of these patients engaged in singing and bible study, still standing 6 feet apart.

We have now become their family, the only faces that they see period, the ones they wake up to and go to bed with. It prevailed to share the words of comfort God present was in that place.

Chapter 6 Online

On our way home one of my coworker told me in the twilight I will be heading to glory, a place prepare for me with beautiful white rose and lots of angels welcoming me home, I think that she was hallucinating due to the current situation we have to live with its endanger even the pets in our home and the animals at various zoo. It was 6:31 she dropped me at my apartment we wave goodbye then she drove off, not knowing that the next day when I showed up at work she would not be there with me we become earth astronauts as I hurry upstairs just to get out of my uniform disinfect and sanitize my shoes I put my clothes straight in the washing heat up my water then take a long hot bath eat my leftover pray headed straight to bed because I got to catch the bus in the Morning good night foes.

Chapter 7 Invaders

Thursday bright and early I am off to work only 6 of us seated on the vehicle as soon as I walking to the time machine to clock in standing across from the front desk I hear someone calling me Emma, Emma I look around it was Secretary Mrs. Shannon she whispered Christina died the sudden and strange news hit me so hard I wouldn't move shock. Lost for words in disbelief felt like about to faint. I was hot, shaking, perspiring heavily. I recounted my time spent with her death is a curse for all men on earth. It comes to rob, steal, and destroy the life of each and everyone but I remember these words I have a plan to bless you and to prosper you. God will continue to a blessing to who seek him kingdom and live by the ten commandments. free yourself from mental slavery none but ourselves can free our mind Moses reminded the people before crossing the red sea that god promises the people not to worship any god more than my god destruction is upon the land because he didn't comply to live by the word of god disobedient lead us to this great inhumane downfall and leaving us as Christian disappointed I cry to god every day to protect me through this time I tested twice and I was negative despite of this monster continue to reign still battling the scientists seek answer to find a diagnosis to cure Covid19 but I turn to god combining in prayer and fasting that will heal the curse but this too shall be with only 2 person place on the floor each day life will never be the same but we stay focus teaching each other about the word of god and learning to love god more we never flouter but grow weary tired and dismay at time I then come to one conclusion to deal with the situation surrounding this outbreak is to humble myself with prayer I can't change the impossible but I know a man who can some called him Savior but I called him Jesus I used the concentrated olive oil and read psalms 27 and 35 we need spiritual guidance to leads us god has never fail me yet faith is the substance of all things and it live inside of me.

Chapter 8 New Converts

June 4th the reopening of stores, restaurants, salons and various entities to allow the economic scourge to be revamped but life is still standing still for most of the city. We don't realize that nothing can restore life other than God almighty so I continued to pray. I stayed connected with my children via Whatsapp and my parents back home just to ensure that they were safe , all my loved ones still remain here on earth. My siblings in London stay connected constantly my sister who is a Christian also would call and we pray together to god who is the head of our life, and our only hope is in Christ Jesus my grandchild was safe and sound whenever, I get an opportunity I will speak with them also one of my grandchild has a chronic illness sick cell so I cautioned her mom to let her stay at home these days the bible become my closest friend looking the phat, the source to breathe, to live ,and survived in this life. let the light shine all around me. I read more each day gaining wider wisdom, and acknowledge how to handle this devastating cycle of conformism as a journalist reporting about the sad news ripped him apart crying with friends family and their love one it was not easy no matter what The Doctors trying to calm the nation by giving timeline for a cure or vaccine they themselves where puzzle, shockingly the minds of human was once disturb millions of death struck the world leaving us with doubt to when this will ended, Jesus only you Lord can stop this pandemic the weeping of the world is like an wolves crying in the darkness our life humid, gray, useless I pray to our father which is in heaven because this shall come to pass if we awaken to the voice of god then blessing will come upon our land. Christian should practice what they preach.

Chapter 9 Inflations

Exhaustion and fatigue leads to mourning everywhere; lots of people's savings have depreciated due to financial pressure, exhalation, failure to reproduce enough wisely, family breakdowns and poverty overtaking the nation. The world is falling apart right before my eyes and marriages are destroyed, children have become scared of living. The school board wouldn't make a prediction to when school reopen, a boy said that was wondering if he can play with his friends again , but I believe that there is a light at the end of the tunnel .Time is ticking the hands of the clock is spinning fast a year running quickly hungry, shortage of food on the table, cry for help, eviction is taking place everyday home owner unable to pay mortgage, car payment too, the lack of humanity help seem hopeless leaving family committing suicide weeping of death throughout the entire world. Congress confused to what must be done, lord have mercy I continue to pray night falling fast the atmosphere change becoming stagnant a trail of misery's lock of comfort some many unrested facing us on a daily basis Furthermore problems continue back at the facility family member still in limbo, waiting for words to when they can start visiting their loved ones who were isolated, it was sad to see them hurting but all of us were in the same situation of life.

Chapter 10 Oxtails

My daughter would say to mommy it
was hard. I responded to a girl I know.
The LP Nurses work twice harder than
before, pushing hours on top of hours,
but they press on with good grace,
depending on lord for strength to do
this challenging job. Door slamming,
phone ringing, it's just confusion all
over the building, the alarms going off
residents wanting to get home, we have

to run checks always to make sure that we have no elopers. It's lunch time we served cream of broccoli soup bake potatoes, with steamed white fish, and Jello for dessert, our count breakdown we now have 14 people to serve as I mentioned before that 3 people died so fast I couldn't imagine it, the administration staff work intensity due to new guidelines and policy that must be carry out by Mr. Covid19, the chief commander, the community undergo a lot of challenges, but we are fighting. Strangely visitor from nowhere appear at the facility causing riot, disruption, invading us like a tornado literally forcing himself inside to see his relative what a crisis the police had was to come and calm those people down this change took many people almost a year to understand this deadly monster, peace restored and everything returned to its usual way things were quiet for that few minutes what a scenery very frighten for the family there were left without options. I walked to my unit and some of the residents were just chilling in the activity room watching television. Supply was getting low, management team but a logo in front of the building (Hero work Here), sometimes I wonder how we do it with short staff persons not showing up for work leaving me to double my feet hurt, my stomach pain, my head hurt, most of our residents is incontinent but only God knows how I did it, but I continue to talk with God for inner strength. Supplication, dedication, determination allow me to prepare myself mentally and physically by taking my vitamins one call alive and drinking a lot of water. I sometimes forget that I didn't eat. At the end of my shift I walk to Walmart 3 minutes from the job and catch my bus home. I sat and thought about how my life events are unfortunately an uncertain death right in front of my eyes to ensure that I wear my facemask shield always. While on the bus I kept my distance knowing that I am Covid19 free, watching the traffic moving along rapidly silently praying to god in my mind I sing how great thou art it's my interaction with the spiritual world help me to stay strong with only my daughter by side, my only desire is to secure her from this destruction of sin, immortality but on immortality we stay true to our maker and we remain humble in Christ Jesus, this new awakening teach me to glorified God more than ever, gosh my unconditional love for God prevail in me, when I go out and come in I wonder why the world began to fall apart its erosion crumbles, break family apart, sinking like the Titan. I remember my journey to Alaska sailing on the great Atlantic Ocean the huge icebergs, enormous whales, dolphins, and seals crying like a child lost in the wilderness, terrible memory that haunts the family who left behind to ride out their storm, extremely difficult in disbelief no flying going or coming in from port to port, ridiculous how life turn out to be in the 20th century mean cruel, heartless, circumstances we are in only living by faith. High tide shipping docking in water with thousands of workers and tourist unable to keep in touch with their love one even the ocean miserable, this pandemic is worse than going across the Bermuda Peninsula, rough and rugged tides rises high its ugly face uncontrollable only the thought remain in our minds of when these crew workers make it home. Great impact leads to depression, causing anxiety, and the death demon continues to reign throughout the world. Being single and divorce for 8 years separate from a man that me and my daughter shared a home with, I was left to stand up in the Gideon and fight this pandemic for me and my daughter. New development is taking place, life transforming and more people becoming true believers of Christ even though. The church doors are closed and we continue to pray significantly. People are clinging more to God and crying out to God to heal the world.

Chapter 11 The Rush

I remember the race for toilet paper and water I just sit back and watch them some people been arrested by the Fort Pierce Police the bible can't lie and the gospel must continue to spread in the land, there is a song with lyrics "because he lives I can face tomorrow" oh yes I get up each morning over myself with prayer at nights I would cuddle up with my daughter, kiss her, and let her know how precious she is. We've been Baptist. At the age of 9 she already knows the Lord from an early stage in her life so she prays always. She is now 11 years old and her faith is spontaneous. The love that she got for the lord is one that speak passion, our journey is amazing one full of gratefulness, powerful fill with anointing in our life, adoring Jesus Christ the Lord and Savior to whom giveth life this is our thanksgiving to God for keeping us away from all harm and danger during these perilous time. She is a Christian who was taught to wait upon the lord, bible study every

1st Wednesday in Jamaica with our Pastor Mckay from the Belle castle Baptist Church. We are from the rural community where she grew up in the beautiful parish of Portland. Every Tuesday we invite Jehovah's Witnesses to come and share the word of hope. Gathering knowledge of the bible was a tremendous validation to mold our spiritual belief with God who created us, however she was excited to learn about Christ and his life here on earth. I can remember frankly when she was only 6 years old at the time after the separation between me and her Dad. On Sunday she takes the taxi all by herself to visit the Kingdom Hall and spend 2 hours at the meeting. I would get words of her participating in the question and answer section, I was elated she was reading brilliant and began to excel in school more and more she achieved 15 medals in track and field then join the netball, l and football team and Pageant show at her school Mini Miss Seaside and came 5th placed. Nagenia got save at a tent crusade close by our house on a Thursday night June 21st 2018 I was surprised when went up on the podium the preacher then ask where is the parent for this child I said here I am pastor she said plainly I want to serve the lord, she took her oath and was Baptist that same night miraculously the angel in heaven where rejoicing another soul for God's kingdom, that very week 4 of us out of the family was Baptist the bible said that a child shall lead the way, and yes she did I give god thanks for saving me my life only get complicated after I runaway to USA but thank God I found a new awakening the life that generate true strength, resentments, restorations, and peace. I challenge it all and build an empire surrounded by the power of faith. My interaction with God plays an essential role in my endeavor to continue to live a splendid life. I am not rich in money but I am rich in Christ. I live by this motto. I can do all things through Christ who strengthens me. Christian today sometimes lose their way and be slaves of men and women that are far from god. I try to live everyday according to my expectations of life. I do not crave material things. I wear simple natural hair and my heart is pure as gold. I don't criticize other of the choice they make in life or who they live because 7 brothers 7 different minds but I appreciate me for who I am today I ask God to continue to protect the life of those person who in isolation and strengthen them for they have lost their love. I believe in healing and power of principalities in high places let us remember our relationship with God one that is honorable, eat well, feed your body with the most important food here on earth which is the bible go out in the world and preach it let not forget that miracle is still working in the life of other people who is in Christ Jesus our soon coming king. Failure is not an option in my life, I walk by faith and not by sight, if we only trust God this pandemic will get under control let God continue to bless you, there is a great change coming I personally accepted Christ in your life I await the day when I can said it is well with my soul a deliverance is coming, when Jesus rose on the third day the only person who see him was Mary Magdalene and the gardener, Jesus relieve is self to her before going to his father heaven, he cause out 7 demons out of a sinner and it when in the swine so I want to say don't let shame and pride stop you from coming to Jesus confess your sin, and walk in the holiness of Christ you will be make whole again. Live your life for Jesus he is worthy to be praise, don't   let go off God unchanging hands learn to forgive and you will prosper, there is no repentance in the grave, if you die with this disease Mr. Covid19 and never confess of your sin here on earth God will be your judge.

Chapter 12 Messy

I want to be ready when He comes, I am preparing to meet my Savior, when the trumpet of the Lord shall sound and the dead in Christ shall rise I pray that I will be the first to behold Jesus face to face, he sheds his blood and Calvary crosses me. These are some bible quotes "Seek him first and all others shall be added unto you", so be ready for the judgment. I am without

fear I am a true inspiration of
scarification, with kind generosity am
serving my God I am a child of the
king, never divide god love in life and
death let the angel encamp around us,
let me fly high like an eagle soaring to
new high spreading my wings out lust
as a peacock, never lose hope heaven
will open up his gate for you be of good
courage and wait upon the Lord. My
hope is built on nothing less but on
Jesus Christ on is righteousness I
believe in one god he will hold me
closed in his arm, and consoled me I
will meditate on his precepts and show
respect in my ways, shelter me o god
hide from this pandemic in you shall I
find refugee life is not easy whatever
come to challenge us let be firm
steadfast, brave ready to fight I urge
 everyone who is broken to make a
covenant with Jesus Christ and come to
the father now he who t seek is grace
shall be saved except a man be born
again he shall enter into the kingdom
of god though he was dead yet shall he
live once more the god of host is with
Lord and Savior, the great messiah
reign in my soul today am fill with the
holy ghost. I want to tell the world that
Jesus is the answer, for the world today
he has though me not to worry about
tomorrow is provide for itself, teach the
children how to pray from a tender age
their a song said, earnestly tenderly
Jesus is calling, calling for you and for

me he said come home he who is weary
come home God don't reject his chosen
one come as who are if you are thirsty
come join hands and heart all over the
universe lets unity as one run to Jesus
now prepared yourself because Jesus is
coming again to rescue the souls of men
I am is sheep once I was lost but now
and found, praise be to God for
favoring me its optimistic the way
things evolve around us, be honest,
thoughtful furious and get right God,
he is not change, he is the same
yesterday, today, and forever let the
lord touch us all today our father in
heaven, in this critical time of
uncertainty, bless us in a special way
strengthen us in your faith visits our
friends, family, neighbors and even our
 enemies be their hope provide for them
lord, open windows, and doors that
shut and comfort those who are
mourning keep us safe, to the world let
nothing prevent from serving god he is
the author and the finisher of our life.
he sit high and watch below in him we
shall find divine healing, worship him
in spirit ,and in truth, he is our great
physician, the only healer ,subscriber to
his channel, log to his website download
the app call life, if hear is word
hardened not your heart, talk to him in
silent, he will break the yoke of
bandage and set the captive free ,he is
my strong tower, walk in his footsteps
,choose life, choose God, build a

relationship now more than ever, I need you oh lord ,I need thee ever hour I need thee. My days are golden now, 2 years have passed its revival time, the rain has stopped, the sun is shining brightly, the sky is blue once more is calm and relaxing, a breath of fresh air, amazingly beautiful. I see the flowers blooming again, the birds flying around, the raccoon eating their food from the garbage, people up and down on the streets wearing their face masks trying to shield and hide this ridiculous stranger who certainly does not welcome Mr. Covid19. Autumn there's this new awakening approaching Jesus will resorted peace in the land gradually as long as human beings obey his words he will keep us safe lord may the love of Jesus be with us all, in a special way my peace I leave with you, my peace I give unto you God bless you all amen. The demonstration make it way across the south of Florida wow more than 150 persons took the streets on Saturday I'm not against it segregation who happening long years ago and it their constitutional right to march no one care about social distant they are seeking justice I hurried home not taking any part of this the wind blowing wildly it was very hot I started to have unnatural thought of this unpleasant sight and how things are going to unfolded in the end of this pandemic particularly in the states where loathing and killing is going I push myself away from it all I keep the bible in my head mash potatoes hot and spicy chicken homemade lemonade I fix this delicious dish for me and daughter I called out to here come over her she run from her room and said mom I can smell the curry chicken I am going to enjoy it we sit at the dinner table we eat our heart out after dinner I do the dishes then dry them thunder clicking wind howling I close lights and in a little while we went into the bedroom I crack the window open it look like a freak storm is coming I was tired with so much going on it scary now we play a pop up game hug my daughter I told her that I love her my eyes was fill with eye no one understands the interchange that is diving the world lord I continue to pray for peace this is a war with Mr. Covid19 doing is thing not pardoning no I am not to put myself in harm's way let them say that am a coward I can live with the fact is I will never let my guard down I will keep my distant it's almost time to go to bed we brush our teeth and dive where in sleep it was each day I would write my prayers and meditate on the greatest gift that god have to mankind I would talk to myself until I fall asleep.

Chapter 13 Restoration

Good morning my dear I said to the child she proudly said good morning mommy. I said it my day off would like to go for a walk after breakfast mom what for breakfast your favorite fry dumplings ,ackee ,and saltfish with hot chocolate tea , nice am going to enjoy I say I know that you will that a Jamaican special and our national dish back home oh I remember my mama making chocolate tea for us on Sundays lord you would lick those fingers none stop putting on a red and white dress v neck with my white sandal I was in a good mood life is become terrifying unemployment plaque the universe nagi dress simple just a in a yellow jean white T shirt and her bright yellow sneakers she take out the garbage on our way the dumpster piling up . I wonder if the truck come around again, I can't of anything except that it was still damp and a little bit wet from the rain last night the chicken strolling slowly like they have no care in this world the pool look so dirty from a distance lord everything has come to stand still like a stubborn mule we walk over to Dairy Queen and sit on outside of the restaurants watching the cars bus trucks and van going you and done what a sight. I could smell French Fries, chicken from inside people going in and out it was quite a business morning we spend half an hour then we headed on home it wasn't worthwhile sitting there anymore this new awakening that hit the entire world I have come to one conclusion today that life demand so much more than to value ourselves and teach us to become each other keeper. I bounced my toe didn't do accidentally but I was hoping along the way to the house 5 minutes away. My daughter was laughing then she turned to me and said sorry mom, it was intentionally we both began to laugh it wasn't one of best days but we make the most out of it irresistible but devastating the fight for life continue while some people recovering from this unwelcome stranger in our midst of life some are gasping for breath and dying I told my girl baby God know man purpose he created us in his our likeness and before we were born he had plan for us home at last I soak my foot with warm water and epsom for a while it was swollen a bit not paining me to much what a relief religious doctrine became reality before the Christian who once read the words of the bible and have to accept the change of not going to mass Sabbath and Sunday service it was live stream congregations stop gathering together no offering and tithes coming in that must I never miss that fact that I was going my body was the true I worship my god none stop pastors evangelist bishop and priest question nationally when will the curfew break and the

Churches will reopening again in our states the war continue people minds was dying gradually leaving the soul to quiver rapidly more sickness taken the land even though the great cry for healing continue live or dye the quarantine shock up everyone with home schooling and line miserable children of life this is a sense of anxiety rocking the children lifestyle it a change that is hard to aspect I wasn't surprised because these are perilous time and I brace myself to acknowledge the circumstances Christ Jesus said "fear not for I am with you" its June 3, 2020 we have to return all school property and collect the year book I am so glad it's almost summer am going on the night shift 3-11pm temperature taken and record water crest it was it was quite in memory care I took my receipt to my manager to get my tuition reimbursement I fill out the paper rush to clock it wasn't my favorite place in the world but it my job glad to see my resident I wash my hands pray to god for taking me check on them then set my tablets for dinner while my coworkers place the clothes in the laundry this was an enormous nursing home with house 94 residents in totally some days you spend their is truly fascinating fun and fill with amusement the charge was their too I have to report my finding ensure that everyone temperature was done and none

recording and high fever no one
missing from the pack the evening
move like rocket 8 pm bedtime
everyone was tucked its was accident
free to suspicious or unusual to be
report on my break I would listen to
Benny Hinn Preach ,this will comfort
my soul life has a new cycle its
adjustments leave strain on us the way
our job usually conducted that no more
very miraculously I am alive Mr.
Covid19 feel threaten some way
somehow because I was always hiding
from him he was my greatest enemies I
believe in one faith and it give hope to
live and fight this death demons which
attack family friends and demolished
happy home there are angel standing
on the battle field guarding God
children notice how its circle the world
crashing into human territory like
Frankenstein what a darkness upon the
land lord I prayed I think twice of what
if I heard screaming and shouting
coming from room 5 I rushing just in
time to see the aide trying to put the
resident clothes but I was raging mad I
had was to get the charge nurse and my
director to come and handle the
situation o lord I left to fold the washed
clothes and pack them away in their
closet the books was update my
coworkers so that enable me to
complete the day task was this a stuck
down for the universe god strike Paul
on its way to Damascus to show his that

he shall obey him I was glad when I
seek the Lord I will not Marvell about
this peculiar world I know it going to
be some touch time am ready to carry
on oh yes I can took a while how to
learn how the to smile so glad I can't
stop crying now I am free to live I can't
denied the true that because of thing
that man on earth have no control of
tackle us like this food banks full all
around I had was to stock up my
pantry also in USA doubt and
uncertainty facing everyone some still
haven't received stimulus check and no
word about the second round will come
our way challenges we face now we may
encounter in the future our daily bread
mention in it April article it said in
proverbs 16:24 gracious word are a
honeycomb sweet to the soul and
healing to the bones Jesus we are your
children we need your instructions lord
guide us and give us wisdom to
overcome unknown destiny Jesus I seek
thee lord I humble myself with
simplicity because today I can say lord
your love conquer all June 8th 2020 its
new moon the sky light up colorful
bright orange shade in between gray
white clouds sailing magically appear
as fire rockets popping and starlight
flashing what an amazing site god
wonderful creation I can imagine the
astronaut floating on mercury or Venus
lovely from where I stand with my head
looking up it was beautiful so

incomparable to anything that I see before only this light show me a promise of hope I walk back to my apartment knowing that god care its new time Mr. Covid19 exposing himself more the cases increase again he is too bold attacking all age race color he hit anyone that is in the way no partially he is a disgrace to the human race Florida see it ugly face increasing 966 new case of Mr. Covid19 leading up to a 1,000 more infected world health organization can to call for the tonic to curl tail him social distant to me he is magnet economic continue to go downhill seems like we are heading in a recession.

Chapter 14 Fulfillment

stock market down dollars deprecating drop gas lower at the pump at the boatyard, yacht and other large fishing vessels rocking from side to side no business was taking place at this pointed time where is my God surprise the fast food franchise are the only establishment growing there are feeding the communities in and around the state my hats go off to them the hard working and dedicated men and women who stand in faith work hours to keep the city open up in time when fear take they stand and fight we are heroes back at work the main dining room remain close the mop look old and shaky him not doing a good job anymore laugh the broom are not sweeping the corners clean either lord Covid19 is killing everything spirit lord have much it serious bad the painting hanging from the wall crying for some color the washing machine always a break down due the amount of laundry we have to do daily normally the resident family would collect the dirty belongs ensure that they are wash and take the back that nothing happening again Jesus keep me calm staff meeting today at 2:45pm we all sit and wait to hear the news at our workplace new policy some of was mumbling around wondering what the changes will affect us I always pray so I leave it to god to secured my job for our Manager came and say good news first or bad everyone said good new it was covid19 never bad like him negative as hell we laugh and laugh he didn't get one positive we all tested negative cheers and clapping as much as we are from different race culture background we hope that we all have our job thank god we did we kick Covid19 ass one side within 10 minutes the bad news it we must be screen everyday single day before commencing our job at Water Crest and we must stop invade the door we all must come to the front desk but we question about extra protective grease we were information that they

are here only how this unpleasant man
don't let we have to use because of him
pandemic we leave the community
feeling relax its was a joyful day for
everyone life continue slowly but surely
social media taking over the world
keeping family and friends together so
many have gone a head but we who are
here must stand in the liberty of Christ
I live by these words I can do all things
through Christ who strengthens me
what a rocky road so many obstacles
blocking the new generations of youth
from enjoying their youth days it hurt
the opportunity of marching at their
graduation hugging and kissing each
dreams to some have ended university
students won't be able to finish paying
of loans parents mind becoming a time
bomb but I say to you press on with
God I do it for me and I know he can
do it for you and you imagine this a life
in paradise I know that if I was given a
chance I would choose life over death
or death where is thy sting oh grave
where is my victory our life here on
earth is through the manifestation of
Jesus Christ our lord what an eclipse
my mom always say to us why worry
when you can pray God is in control
loud bang tire bawling on St. Lucie
west crowd scattering boom the a
sudden silent it was a silver Honda run
off the road into the busy shopping
center of Walmart another screaming
coming from the inside of the crash

vehicle I stared in disbelief I would
recognize a woman voice and a child
crying the lady is saying I can't move
someone a tall white man rush out to
the scene with more persons trying to
pull them from the cruel up Honda it
was an accident right in front of me you
can hear the fire truck coming and the
flashing light of port St Lucie police
they allotted from the unit as quickly as
possible they get the child out first then
they had was to cut out the woman
from front seat she was pin between
the steering wheel and the air bag I try
not to get too close I was waiting on the
route 6 bus it was running behind
schedule the police was assisting the
ambulance team the bus is here I have
to hop on I wouldn't let my ride leave
me it my only been of getting we
departed within 7 minutes leaving this
gruesome and terrifying bloody
unfortunately time I was always
picturing Jamaica Lord I keep on
hearing the voice of the child crying I
try to forget it out of my mind I
remember me and my cousins roasting
breadfruit climbing ackee tree going to
river playing church and mama and
papa I miss home and the family
support that I use to been am so tired
if my mom was here my dinner would
cook. should make for me some oxtail
,boil banana, and dumplings you
 would lick your fingers hot and spicy
seasons with dry pimento berry,

scallion, thyme, garlic, scotch bounty
 pepper, ginger, and Jamaica most
 famous jerk seasoning, meat melting
off the bone soft juicy and tender we
love mummy food our cultural if totally
one of a kind our authentic dish super
delicious not to mention our fashion
and dance move more and more my
heart is becoming longing for home as
we reach my next change over to the
route 1 one bus I skipped across like a
busy kangaroo my foot wobbling dying
to sit down the driver waited for
another 3 minutes it was only 4
passenger on board all keeping
treasure coast guideline 6 feet apart
from each I hang my head down rest
my chin in the palm of my hands so
exhausted after a few stop then the next
stop was mines I got it was sand at port
St Lucie at last as I enter the apartment
complex there was a bus mark bright
bites my vision was draw to see this
colorful bus drawing of kids fruits and
vegetables on both side wow it replace
the rainbow its almost 4:15pm they
were 2 ladies standing around a small
gray table with 2 igloos on the ground
of the one of the lady call out to me
miss you got child I said yes a little I
walk over and she handed me a bag I
tell

her thank and hurried across the
volleyball court I am a feet blocks away
from home when enter the staircase I
hush up so fast reaching in my bag for
my key thank god am home too horrid
I stretch out on floor to ease the tension
in my back so much I my little girl
come into my bedroom she said
mommy why are lying there I said baby
girl pain she said hush mom she join
me and we hug each my God I couldn't
believe the time that I wake it 9:17pm
lord give me strength I have never sleep
this long ever since I know myself I cool
off then took a cold shower put my
uniforms to wash I was curious to see

what the lady gave me in the bag.

Chapter 15 Reunite

I just get an opportunity to open inside
was 2 box of milk 1 small orange a
welch peanut butter and jelly sandwich
in plastic container with peach and
some Cheerios a plain white plastic bag
with small baby carrots it was a
complete meal breakfast and lunch Mr.
Covid19 is causing significant food
crisis in our community most family
remain unemployment I was grateful I
continue to pray to god my daughter
prepared Macaroni and cheese for
dinner I sit and eat just enough to
contain me I was so bless that I still
have a job and was able to fend so my
entire family the answer to this crisis is
caring I drink a lot of water to keep my
body going like a car engine 25 came I
place my wash clothes in the dryer lord
life has really upside down the world is
in fear I brace myself for any strange
my spirit told me this night to what the
Jamaica I turned the television on hit
Youtube by watching the a lady dress
in a pink dress came on she was shot by
some solider on operation in the
community of August Town St Andrew
I paused it then and pause it over and
over for about 6 times she was my dear
friend lord I cried and cried our life is
so miserable I started to pray Almighty

god ruler of heaven and earth we need
your intervention gracious father we
have been rob by death demons the
shadow of evil has attack innocent
father am a true believer I need to her
from you lord hide me from the snare
and the hands of the wicked lord am
hungry for you our father bring peace
now Jesus comfort my soul father open
our blind eyes we are lacking vision of
you Jesus we need you Jesus Christ you
did so that we can have life abundantly
but the devil try to kill us all your flesh
and blood was shed for me lord give me
wisdom and understanding to walk by
faith there's a power in your name
bless and preserved my life you are the
same yesterday and today the storm
will ended when humanity chose you
rescue us Lord rescue us I thank you
for you grace amen I couldn't stop
crying I watch the news again she was a
special woman her life cut short just
like that crime have taken over our
island saddened by her passing I
remember all those time that she was
caring for my little a very good clean
neat and tidy words can't express who
we miss you my dear sleep well until we
meet again I didn't know how to break
the news to my baby girl I hug her then
I said someone back home die a person
whom you love dearly she said
grandma I said no its shanti she said
mom the soldiers must be charge for
her death I said let god be the judge the

outcome another killing omg God life a young man I meet while working in Kingston Jamaica is death on the guns continue to riddle the body of trying inner city youth mothers bawling blood running east Kingston nervous it war in the city no future I couldn't talk I become speechless rivals gang turning on each other covid19 produce more rampage hungry confusing and distress some many life shamble I never witness anything like this it's a dry and windy morning I get a cup of lime ginger and garlic tea take my medications and relax I have to live my life one day back on the slavery just to make an earning I am barely surviving but I never complain about nothing I ride with the tide hours cut again for this week I know for me and my house hold we will continue to praise god always it quite around here checking up on the garden outside the rearranging of the plant by one of our resident the petal look lovely and they wasn't dead they were fresh and looking god is blessing even the flower at the work place Joan make sure that she water them each day if we feed our minds with the word of god we would flourish just like the plant in the garden I never hear from my cousin since she told me about Shane's death my day was always the same nothing soft music playing in the building before it quite if a pin drop you or you could hear we have to

45

allow god to shine is light in this our dark situation even when like it at is darkest like great Israel we can find comfort in knowing god destruction has come upon the land I try not to think about it but continue my journey for when am exhausted I sing hymn of praise and enjoy what my job it hard to see them suffering I praying silence this prayer echoes forgiveness for human been sin because he are not perfect o Lord remember not only the men and women of goodwill but also those of ill I began to make my last rounds before leaving it 2:45 pm I went to room 5, I hear the residents gasping for breath from is bed I call him by name but is chest racing so fast I went back and get the charge nurse I uttered Jesus is pulse rating later increased also as a gentle husband to his beautiful my inner spirit told me that he is journeying I see death right in front my eyes is color changing blood pressure high the nurse told me that she will be giving him oxygen we attached th into is nasal wash our hands nurse leave while she w began to connect moment has God's kingdo mystery but we always fits with Romans 8:27. The and I was very quiet I know that he was de

gone softly and we leave the room I
shook my head in a moment when we
the greatest need was to simply
acknowledge now what the spirit
intercede we are no match to handle life
on own our father has ascended up into
heaven to his father house where he has
prepare a place for all of us who dead
in Christ when the resurrection come
and trumpet of the lord shall sound and
they who die in the lord shall see him
first o my god what a promise god
doesn't require us to be dauntless in the
face of adversity but instead invites us
to come to him with our questions so I
didn't pressure myself to come to
strange conclusion of what causes room
5 death I trust God always I informed
my coworker about the lost I express
myself without despair.

Chapter 16 Back On Track

I struggle to accept death I clock out I
have a severe headache I thought it was
migraine or maybe it was my sinus
acting up while am walking am saying
to myself before crossing the busy
streets of California dear father when
doubts and fear overwhelmed me help
me to remember that I am precious in
your sight I forget Watercrest as soon
s I exit the building I breathe deeply
rns tooting people going in different
ctions in went to Walgreens and

buy a bottle of Tylenol 500 for pain I
had water in my bag so I take 2 I reflect
on how great our God is the Lord
giveth and the lord has taken away may
the name of the lord be praise job
1:12pm. Saturday afternoon was my
day off my family time me and my
daughter stop at a local restaurant for
lunch as the waitress set a fresh bowl of
chicken salad crispy fries and a thick
burger on our table my daughter asked
her what his name we pray as a family
before we eat we pray for everyone who
are suffering especially for those who
lost their love one due to Mr. Covid19
she said mom I will pray today learning
from our little ones it delight me how
brave and bold children nowadays are
she said lord I thank today for life as
we journey in fear cover us lord
provide for the hungry and the family
who are suffering heal them Jesus let
him seek you dear lord and all give
them peace lord I thank you for this
day I pray amen he have a wonderful
time down came the rain again after
holding up for a few day now th
were huge more than 3inch
fall on the streets wate
running swiftly in
we had to sit fo
inside the restau
with pink lemona
call my sister in Lo
and her family is doi
good we were trying h

about the murder earth secret spy and killer bad boy Covid19 she said sis people a try all kind a ways to get rid of him them used cleaning agent household products they now introduce drinking ginger lime turmeric apple cider vinegar with cayenne pepper onion and garlic we couldn't help laughing ginger and garlic with ginger lemon tea bag and 2 paracetamol London reopening school in June and she have no choice but to returned to work none of sibling or my nieces and nephew was attack by the outer space killer no one thank be to go Covid19 bad he is unstoppable but me not going to let him win we ended the conversation on the contrary I still believe Mr. Covid19 is going to die but it going to take some time with no fix date in Washington people are waiting to hear if the will be a second round of stimulus package coming I know that life has change and it won't be the same too much catastrophes drama dream look dry up anyway we walk back to 7 eleven gas and buy 2 Hershey's chocolate bar and wait for our taxi to drop of home my daughter wanted crab so I stop by win Dixie to get her some when she see the large toes she whisper mom that not crab in Jamaica crab don't look like that I knew real crab Lord Jesus I wanted to curried it for her we call it back home crab to Marley se grater a dry coconut juice it season up with your hot pepper scallion onion thyme and garlic I used the first time Indian curry and turmeric boil some banana and served it hot she was scared of the even the color of the crab legs it was bright orange I laugh until I crack up I said Jesus if you're not busy please talk a walk into win Dixie she pull me away so I left without get the crab lord have mercy we are here thanks driver it was a little bit cooler now it feel like 70 degree after the rain nice did Covid19 have an army with him world invasion who remember the Jetsons transportation that how covid19 and is troops can you imagine how vicious they all the animals are dying money can't save life anymore trust and hope so I continued to praise god when I see all these welcome behavior by the fellow something tell me that he is truly the death demon sweeping through the hemisphere we need a break through seriously Mr. Covid19 stops the killing now. We are heartbroken I keep on living on God promise to heal our land, this pandemic ruined some parts of my life separat loves everyone every tomorrow promise to none of we are i uncertain time Mr. Cov taking no deal beca right death toll cont 2020 new figure on th can't hide the wings of g covering I have to face the

day this mean man wicked I was thirsty
I have a bottle of eat a apple I hate
watching the news these last days a
revolution is here people are desperate
I live a humble and sacred life I finish
packing my bag for work arranging my
closet setting my alarm for later clean
the bathroom and changing my bed
vacuuming the house to keep my mind
from thinking about this situation it
also another 14 days and I have to get
tested Monday morning before I leave I
hate the feeling of this sob going up my
nostril it hurt I can't stand it but I
really don't have a choice because my
bills have to paid I carry that weight all
by myself no husband no boyfriend I
am my financial accountant I have to
do the math on my own my eyes get wet
whenever I have to take Mr. Covid19
tested sometimes I said God dammit if I
could just walkway but we become a
prisoner now we have to face the law I
know am clean am never after of the
results that was coming back from the
health department. 801 apartment an
elderly lady live here I visit her for the
first time I help her to take some
grocery I saw her from a distant
walking with 2 big shopping bags she
stop and rested for a while I said mom
would like some help she reply thank
you I lived at 801 I said find u will
never see me walking slowly I am a
 mover always on the move I got their
before I waited around 6 minutes for

her she introduce herself and I do the same we talk and she asked me if I am a Christian I told her yes I was first marriage in the seventh day Adventist but later I got Baptized in the church in a small community in Jamaica its name is Belle castle in the parish of Portland she said I am from Kingston I was happy to be meet you mom she said likewise she had an English ascent I could tell that she was in London because I was there too she told about a church after you past the railroad on Edwards road and she asked me where in the complex am living I told her Building B she gave her number and said that I can come by sometimes with my daughter I told her that I must run now my little girl was at home I was happy that I could be of help to someone when I came home I share the good news with my child we sit outside on the veranda just to relax and get some fresh air with no school work to do we would play dominoes Uno sliders and color and paint together no to be get boring we enjoy each other company so much I have some marinate chicken in the refrigerator I steam some vegs with boil potatoes and brown stew chicken whenever I stay long inside she would asked mom what are you doing we have a great time I love avocado served with celery broad bean and beetroot no honey mustard I squeeze fresh lime juice with olive oil on mines I try to stay healthy and eat right my weight is 149 pounds I maintain an average body shape and size God favor me for dessert we have cheese Danish ring it was good not too sweet my drink was water I work hard so I drink a lot of water can afford to get dehydrated. The clock on the wall ticking the time is running faster than I can imagine I immediately check my email to see if I got any important messages I respond to a few that need urgent notification I reread some of my junk mail nothing new my school was pay my internet and my pay hit my bank account everything was ok life is more than a jigsaw puzzle hard to find the piece it just unbelievable surprisingly no one let that matter the greatest thing I got a job and that what count terrifying but coping well regardless of the way how it seem my world is magical the beach is crowed these days when I was growing my summer was excited lots of wild grapes honeycomb ripe bananas coconut water roast fish and boat ride a big almond tree with a swing make with one tire a piece of rope hanging a low so everyone can reach my father would have party on the beach it was fun I was the baby my brother taught me how to swim and catch fish we would ride skateboard up and down we the inseparable children today play video games and control social media for me I was fortunate to

enjoy my childhood Mr. Covid19
you're an obstacle to children I pray
for you not to get depress it will get
better let our father in heaven fix it
parents let stand and encourage them
to continue to make the best of life it
have its value life will be restored the
peacock walk patiently and unveiled its
tail with pride the falcons walk upright
showing proper morals look how slowly
it move respect other stick with your
goal don't be fooled by this uninvited
quest that display grieved pain and
angry in everyone life some way or
another death will stopped one day I
am inspired and convinced there is
hope they will be sunshine in the valley
for me my god die for our sin he drink
vinegar for water I wasn't their when
the nail pierce in his hands we was
wounded for I wasn't their when the
sword went through his side they place
a crown upon on is head to prove to the
world that he is my king there's none
like you Lord I love you Lord great are
you lord we will brought us through
this moment but it will never be the in
the world we has been shaken up
wondering when we are to move
forward I say to you brethren fasting
and praying is the only way of survival
we need a rival to revives us again
Worthy are you lord he will heal the
land if we give him space in our life
think about these things read the bible
and stay connected with Jesus lord

forgive us of our sins touch our life in a special way Jesus we need a miracle o gracious father come to the rescue of men god have a purpose for all of we knew me from I was in my mother's womb Lord I didn't brought me this far to leave me.

Chapter 17 New Opportunities

I will follow the footprint that he left in the sand, I will build my house upon the rock. I need to touch the end of your garment, wash me and make me white as snow purifies me Jesus , just like the woman at the well. To the universe look at you self as a star you are the light in your family eyes never fade away identify your purpose on earth and I know my purpose is to fight on till the end it not over until it over soar high like an eagle race across the finish line Mr. Covid19 must be control by consuming fire he will shrink from the heat he will die slowly look at is now he is a bragger but soon become a flogger how long shall the Eden reign. My world crashing it just too frightening Mr. Covid19 stand strong new cases arise more and more trust him too courageous and bare face not even a drunkard can escape from but prayer warriors have to keep on attacking the reckless dangerous cold hearted killer we need to cramp him

style the maroons blowing their Abeng
Rastaman chant Niyabinghi around
fire side Christian and other
denominators worshipping to god in
the own way they used these various
method such as fasting and prayer to
murder the most wanted man on earth
right now but still no luck it is slipper
like a heal but my God is a timely God
he soon capture His victory is mine said
the Lord of host weeping and mourning
throughout the world scientists struggle
to find a hardcore drug to demolished
this unwelcome and notorious stranger
earth invader if not most of the sight
seen area are closed just allow me to
mention a few botanical gardens Disney
land waterfalls historical sight parks
swimming pools but   most tourists
resorts are opening little by little up in
phases no entertainment either bowling
may eventually give us a chance in the
summer with these crippling condition
surrounding our community its literally
causing ache and pains leaving others
in disbelief and distressed no form of
recreational or outdoor activities when
suddenly the doorbell ring as soon as I
open the door it was a brown
cardboard box sitting at the door it was
address to me I was anxious to open it
got a knife a slit the box it was my
toaster I have been waiting on it for 3
days now amazon drop off wow nice
color silver and red I remove it from
the smaller box set it and pull it in its

was working oh yes I knew that I got the right I tossed 2 slices of bread wash my hands and spread it welch grape jelly yummy the jelly dripping I have to chew fast not wanting it to spill on the kitchen floor beautiful and shiny I steam it yesterday and sanitized right through and through with my Jamaican white over proof rum fresh fragrant from air wicked freshener that is pull in and my sofa was also sanitized with breeze fabric cleaner I maintain a well keep house I wasn't too doughy not clean it's my comfort zone so I love my little paradise it's my rata castle I clean all the door knobs too my bathroom clean always after we take our shower with school almost out we had to returned the laptop to the school and collect our year I call the taxi after completing my task and headed over to west k-8 school do the exchange and drive to St. Lucie west on to California Blvd. staff meeting it was we were told now that the next Mr. Covid19 test will be done at a fix date o lord my poor nose I can imagine the fear factor the nostril have now no one have any great concern we know we will have to live with Covid19 for a while but plan are generating how to ambush him what a world we had to sit within the 6feet boundaries no hugs anymore just hi and bye ridiculous right I was thirsty so I asked chef for a glass of fresh apple juice which I water down half and half to my surprise I was call on the demonstrate how to use the gloves and change the protective gown I was a new graduate from nursing assistant school it was so sudden I was in dismay I went up and did my thing I was applauded by my all member of staff I really appreciate the moment no one except this not even my director the meeting ended everyone went their separate ways some back to work while headed home I got a ride to my place of aboard it took me 18 minute to get their the speed trap in the complex was so high for this low kia it look like a 2015 model well keep and smelling good I exit the vehicle said girl see you on Monday we are on the 7am shift together she slowly drive away me taking my own time to walk upstairs I live on the second floor my mind was fix on god am not thinking of the problem that we are facing sometimes they're test paper from our God just like the irregular weather today it was very humid the heat coming from out of the earth was burning my face is bouncing like a cricket coming at batsman with speed faster than a whirlwind it was reversible I hurried inside gosh it feels better inside I always my hands whenever I get home change my working place them in my laundry basket my little girl was away for a day I was some left over plantain and carrot porridge for my dinner I juice my coconut milk grater with my own hands relaxing at home enjoy my company I humble myself as a child I read psalm 91 then turn on the television and watch my favorite series Anne with an E really interested I could stop watching it teenager days was special I wouldn't help to reflect on my childhood really enthusiasm and optimistic how we transform from stage to stage in our life mature early become mothers and fathers and wow we are granny time really fly it was yesterday I was one wishy washy little leaving from preparatory school red and white ribbon in my hair pleated uniform a small wonder woman bag pack on my back at age 13 high school it was so am hock on the film love you self always I look forward to the conclusion of the next series season 3 how Annie try to fit in she was the only girl with red hair she was teased by everyone but in the end she find a quiet place to build her strength she talk to the wind trees and the animals that help her to realized who she is as a person sometimes we all need that break away and meditate that evening was mines to do block my mind from the disaster than drive the whole city in death sadness rage angry loneliness and in despair I pray to the lord I continue to read my bible my daily bread for spiritual connection with our supreme God I pray for the broken family so they will be heal and for god to dry they tears from their eyes this is a world destruction people were falling apart remember our messiah he can calm the storm he is our captain sail with caution look out too many wreckage occurred always ready go easy now the compass along cant land us safely stay focus on the road ahead that lead to life eternity my experience dealing with challenges through the pandemic as Christian I have my guard up fierce like a lion harm and dangerous not taking any chances with Mr. Covid19 I quickly remember these words from the book of Deuteronomy 31 verse 8 the lord himself go before me and will not leave me nor forsake me don't be afraid be not discourage o thank you Jesus I understand God is now me shield in him I shall hide amen I need o Lord I need every I need pass me my gentle Savior Lord I come to thee.

Chapter 18 Happy

I bow down on my knees and cry out to your lord o heaven open your gate and send angels around the 4 corner of the earth my mouth shall always sing praises unto you lord keep our heart and mind in tune some people eyes are looking up to heaven we seek answer lord but you are the ruler of the universe the alpha and the omega the.

beginning and the end the author and the finisher of all things here in heaven on earth Lord fill me up with your grace for its sufficient lord as devastated and confuse has the world only you my god can calm it lord let your light so shine around men give us hope wisdom and understanding lord to cling to more as Lord and Savior to the all of us throughout the land is your thirsty come to Jesus now this the time to seek him there in trouble in the world leaders are brain wash in despair family losing love ones some of penny less o God I cry to everyone to come in his arms which is wide open and waiting for you come the book of David which is psalm 144 says praise be to Lord who is my rock who train my hands for war and my fingers for battle my stronghold my deliver in whom I find refuge who subdue all is people under him is the amazing my god how great thou hart almighty God console now we are miserable in disbelief but is god time we must accept him now today not tomorrow because it not promise to none of we are like a pilgrim passing through this barren land we are only stranger here just for a little while blessed are you lord I sanctified your holy name there is no one like you lord you're an awesome God and you reign I live for you always lord we are pressed on every side by trouble but we are not crush we perplex but not despair 2 Corinthians 4:8 this pandemic come to let us live in fear but I hope everyone learn something for Mr. Covid19 to value this moment treasure the memories and hold to what count make time each day to realized how life is and to thank god for each blessing maybe this pandemic teach us to appreciate what we got and how quickly we can lost it time to live by the 10 commandment especially love one another also care for the living and the dying treat each with respect stop living for ourselves god can get angry too he is upset with us at time if we seek forgiven pray and believe he will heal our land shopping spree for my little we went to goodwill she save $32 so I dedicate you have spent your own money now she has gotten taller and taller overnight she is 4 feet 9 inches she is maturing real fast we were our mask outside and on the shopping mall it wasn't busy at all you would see everyone taking precaution social distance it was ah I was happy to see that people began to realize the true sense of staying alive sales clearance it was the stores are trying to make an extra dollars or 2 to 3 months of not selling anything I can imagine the fashion line remain trendy summer wear in fine style flip flop their excessive amount I am in the kids department 50% off on all items I grab a few items for her next stop rainbow I thought it was the regular opening hours I was stunned 11am lord that unbelievable I continue to eye shop around a few other store more people were going the same obviously I could tell not having money to waste now a days you got to pinch on the little that you got some don't even have a penny to their name time is moving so rapidly my waiting time was weighing in mind secretly could show any facial expression didn't want to disappoint my daughter I have to get ready to catch the bus to go to work different type of brand name clothes place on the anique we stand outside looking through the glass window thank god it is 11 am the store door open we hurried inside quickly she buy a flat blue slipper and I get a black leather sandal paid the cashier and left with such urgency I had no time to eat it took us 9 minutes to walk I drag on my uniform and dash out the front door the bus was predicted to arrive at 12:15 pm I hustle without delay running across US 1 on fort pierce running breathless within 7 minutes I was almost at the my bus stop I was stop again by the train I would hear it blowing from a distant I halt myself at a mini malt close by I was almost on Edwards Road long lines of traffic has to stop also the gate bar was dropping and the red light keep on flashing everything remain neutral I waited another 3-5 minutes to get the

green light I was so fast across from
Emil Avenue and boom there I was at
my bus stop I realized my tension that
was in my head space telling me that I
won't catch the bus as I approach the
area that sometime it is so desolate I got
company 3 men 2 boys and an Indian
its seem like we are waiting on the bus
it 11 minutes past the hour noon time I
look up the busy street to see if the bus
is coming not yet insight it as I turn my
head around again for the second it was
right here the day was so hot I was
sweating water running down my spine
I was soaking wet we all take our seats
and maintaining Mr. Covid19
guidelines I was happy inside the bus
was so cool I was feeling and inhale that
fresh air I observed the boys on their
phone and everyone minding they
business I was undistributed it so quite
a tall young man sitting in the back seat
he was wearing a black T shirt and a
sky blue pant with curly hair eventually
I get to my second stop because I had to
change over am at Rio Mario this heat
hit me again it seems like it 90 degrees
hot like the Sari dessert no breeze the
trees that around stand still you can see
like stress coming of the asphalt no rain
clouds the sky is blue and pretty a lot of
white clouds I wasn't surprised we have
gotten the rain and the thunder flash
flood a few days ago the sun stand still
my number 6 bus has arrived the
driver was wearing is protective gear

he is my friend I greet him and find a seat all the way in the back of the bus my head was 7 watch an increase 4 get off at prima vista stop 2 of the men stand outside smoking talk and interacting with each other no form social distant lord help my only hope that are safe because this killer Mr. Covid19 has no care for now the ride from here to St. Lucie west was very smooth I got off at my stop I was burning up I remember that I got in my bag a bottle of water and an apple so thirsty and hungry I drink the water little by little I need my energy to do my job I never even get to take my vitamins my stomach was empty it was early so I walk back to port St. Court house sit for another half hour then stroll to my work place shift was changing over now took my temperature it was 98.0 and I was handed 2 envelope by the receptionist it was my last pay slip I have forgotten about it completely everything remain the same I clock in and get my review from my coworkers before they go through the down not peculiar happen that would surprise me my director was their she informed us about a new way of doing the resident log sheet of how and when they eat or not eat or shower and don't shower I said ok I got my gloves a few garbage bags and begin to check my residents the nursing station door was close so I didn't know who was on duty I prayed every day for god grace to take me through my 8 hours for shift no accident or incident to occurred so I monitor everyone closely set the table for dinner it my regular routine I get so accustom to these task I never let nothing border me really my time went by and I wouldn't wait to kick I was extremely tired my legs hurt only 2 persons on the floor along the one of the most dedicate one who always chip and help us not everyone is so kind people going on 2 weeks vacations it was crazy no my bestie Jennifer is off starting today I have to fend for myself and find my way to work on Tuesday night now we sure keep in touch she is one amazing woman a woman of faith prime and dignity she self-centered herself with prayer she move like a bullet when we are working together we get the job done quickly we never hitch I am going miss her so much its now 10:45 pm.

Chapter 19 The Crossroad

we check the resident ensure that they
are clean and sleeping in their beds and
no one was up wandering for me it's
time to leave still hot outside oh my god
hmmm it still humid the journey home
was awesome just want to dive straight
in I was home alone my daughter was
staying by my neighbor house until in
the morning I go in read psalm 91 and
use the bathroom then bed it was thank
Jesus for your protection our my life
thank for your guidance you're the
light Mr. Covid19 continue to show off
himself again dangerously he is
enjoying this south Florida has been
jeopardize once total rising rapidly he

is embarking on bad phat I can't wait
for bounty hunter to get a hold of this
bastard so wrecked wicked and
murderous is heart is cold he is
invading everywhere ah time sir they
are preparing some for antidote or
antibiotic soon and God is working he
is slow but sure wait u better watch it
boss he coming after you big time have
fun now you're so disgusting brutal
lord we are depending on you this
battle is for you lord no one on earth is
prefect but lest no submitted ourselves
to this death trap look up to Jesus stay
focus give her life it's your to protect its
a new day with new dawn awaking
breakfast it was pancake scramble eggs
some real lime tea no sugar added with
fresh fruits served with cottage cheese I
pray and asked to bless me I try not
make too much because I cant waste
food in the crucial time a lot of persons
don't have food in their house this not
nice as I eat I pray in my heart for the
world each day seem scary than the day
before my community continue to show
an increase also to Mr. Covid19 what is
causing this no compliance children
are left alone to find way how to
survive any entire family die out in
front of their eyes frightened by this
pandemic upsurges they are confused I
can imagine the emotional impact this
place on them in regard to been along
no family support they system is setup
to place them in foster care now these

children are full traumatized they will need social workers guidance counselor to work with them when they are dark day Jesus with light up their heart he said suffer the little children to come unto we who remain must teach about god and is love for them read bible story with those that are grieving the road is long all we need is time to find comfort in our youth life advise them not to give up life is wonderful just live for Jesus magnify the lord build a relationship with him forget yourself for a moment and talk to him he will work miracle in your life and a change is coming so be confident believe in God faith is the substance of all things and always remember that you can do all things my children through Christ who strengthens you live by the word of God their power in the blood watch god turn our pain into joy tear into laughter and saddened to happiness behold I show you a mystery Mr. Covid19 will die and go back right in the pit of hell where belong be patient is day is fast approaching god will never wipe out a complete city because someone is praying in that city so we shall live and not die and declare the glory of god this death demons rampage will stop only through prayer and fasting discretion will guide you understanding will watch over you proverbs 2:11. The world is changing, streets are empty, so many people are

dying. I asked the people of this world
will you change and choose life more
than death. The book of Revelation
reveals to us all these things that are
happening in our nation today. I am
not astonished by what eyes god is a
spirit and we must worship him in
spirit and in truth just pray to the lord
whenever you get a minute to pray . I
encourage the world to do so trust god
don't let anyone or anything distract
you from praising him we all got a
number in heaven when the host of
angel appear unto us we had to go
home to glory land rejoice I said rejoice
Isaiah `` 41:10 "I will strengthen you
and help you I will uphold you with my
righteous right hand". God is ready to
stand by us always do not fear and he
promised us in "John 10:28 and I give
to them eternal life and they shall never
perish" shall any man pluck them out
of my hands our lord and Savior Jesus
will spare is children only if we obey is
word and seek is face isn't this amazing
I believe in the highest God I love the
lord with my whole heart marvelous is
he wonderful counselor mighty is my
king holy and righteous is he lord I
adore you lord time pass is by no one
can control Mr. Covid19 until this day I
continue to glory my father who is in
heaven I turn my bible and read psalm
5 verse 1 give ear to my words o lord
consider my sighing listen to my cry for
help my king and my god for to you I

pray in the morning lay my request
before you I wait in expectation you are
not a god who take pleasure in evil with
you the wicked I can't dwell Mr.
Covid19 God is the greater king and he
will crush you am waiting too many cry
for help coming from the entire nations
lord heal our land we as Christian fully
understand that our god will stand with
is people and we shall be saved from
the hands of this death demon lord
 remember us oh Israel I will lift up
mine eyes unto the hills whence cometh
my help my help cometh from the Lord
who made heaven and earth thank you
Jesus I know am not worthy of your
praise because we have sin against you
lord forgive and heal our land lord you
said that we are nothing dust we came
from and dust shall we return my life
depended on you lord in you I trust. I
have hope faith and patient that you
will deliver us out of this terrible
pandemic and restored life and give us
peace eternal, lord my heart is not
haughty the moment when life has cut
short and family are broken unable to
hug ,kiss and laugh with each other,
human beings has come to realize we
have to seek you Lord more each and
every day . When the rain fall it don't
fall on one man house top ,this means
that we are all affected by Mr. Covid19
in one way or another. Therefore I shall
pray for the world the lord is my
shepherd I shall not want me makes me

to lie down in green pasture he restored
my soul yea though i walk through the
valley of the shadow of death hide me
under your wings , Lord break the yoke
of chain of bandage and set us free . I
want to be remembered like the woman
of Samaria, my God only the fittest of
the fittest will survive because we are
in the last days. Jesus if it is not your
 will then let it be done, my God am
longing for home this is too unbearable
. There are stars amongst us that
continue to disappear war upon the
land, men becoming lovers of
themselves, the root of money evil ,
material things destroying us, death
stained the universe , this great
awakening leads us to turn from our
wicked ways and serve to seek God
 first and all other things shall be added
unto us. Weeping may endure for a
night , but joy will cometh in the
morning blessed is he that is in lord
 than he that is in the world. Our
father, who is in heaven let's   exalted
his name on high , listen world we
can't go to the father but through our
Savior Jesus Christ which is his son ,
every knees shall bow and every
tongue confess that he is Lord. To my
loved ones , friends, family ,neighbors
and enemies, I know that it a difficult
time for all of us throughout the world
I am here to tell each and every one
 that God loved us don't feel like he
has forgotten us, sometimes he is mad

at the way he see us living but i know that it's scary to accept death . I am proud to be a child of the king don't let the devil attack your mind, stay connected with God he will give wings like eagle so that we can soar, be brave like a lion, bold as a bear think about the olden day when Noah place 2 kinds of every animals on earth in the ark, there was a great flood this pandemic Mr. Covid19 is just an illustration of how God will rescue souls from dying. Take all precaution measures as possible, look after each other and love one another for this is so in the Lord. My peace I leave with you my peace I give unto you love God and live to God be the glory of great things he has done.

Chapter 20 The Life Form

Keep me safe until the storm passes by I continue working at the community testing is done every 14 days that we have to live with nothing change no one missing we stick together looking out for each other I finish school and aiming for high height I let the word of god manifest in me back home in Jamaica my children are healthy and in good condition I spoke with my mom and Dad every Sunday Lord cover them life styles is not the same I focus on things that need to be done on a daily basis. I don't know about you I shall sings praise to god all the day long

I can rejoice my bills are paying and I
still got a job thank god me and my
daughter still together always it
summer and we going to enjoy either
Mr. Covid19 like it or not time sir time
I make myself happy I am smiling I
never feel my world is ended am
breathing am that important its dry
and hot climate change is taking over
too one day when this is over I can look
back and said thank you Jesus this too
must pass I listen to old gospel song
praise and worship and communicate
my inner spirit allowing him to direct
its one year since am in my job today
am inspired by other who are Christian
to challenge my spiritual acquaintance
more with our father in heaven fort
pierce malls and shopping center is
operating each day I watch the people
going and coming without fear I will
not fear my star shining in the galaxy it
represent me it is so bright I become
more wiser than I was a few months
ago my angels are telling me don't give
in to the darkness that cover the earth
maybe the damage is done I can't look
back have to push forward in life with
one goal and one destiny one aim to
stay focus beach day I pack my bag
with fresh fruits water and 2 towel we
catch the bus and off we go no sun
cream just some coconut oil to rub skin
it was sunny temperature is 85 degree
lord have mercy the water was cold the
wave bouncing around at this little spot

was only me and little girl we swim close to shore water not passing our is area that no one go more me and I listen the ocean whistling from a distant the seagulls crying and the white yacht sailing by away from the stress and a break from work we spend our time reflecting on when we were in Jamaica our beach days was fun we make tuna sandwich for lunch and water as usual we play on the shore collecting one by one I didn't stop to check my I complete put it away today is my breathing I really need that space there was a small grape tree near on the left side where it block the view of anyone to see us I enjoy my day around now we get ready change out of those and cold clothes we get dress and begin our walk we stop at a park with a playground my girl was sliding up and down running around was extremely excited she love the outdoors we move again we stop to look at a painting on the wall of a Museum it's a family picture of a mother father dolphin and a baby very interesting this painting share a lot about family which is very important to all of us that why we lose a family member it treat us apart I said my daughter at that isn't this beautiful life itself is beautiful and God make each and every one adorable wow the parents cuddle the young it fin protection the child was an amazing moment we laugh and continue on our way we stop by the cake lady a pastry shop 4 block we went inside the design of the cakes and cupcake lord the wonderful colors let my vision is more clear now wow the craving was fantastic a wedding cake standing on silver platter is was it has 6 layers I never anything like this in my is pretty like a cake heaven my said miss do sell birthday cake the lady point us to an area where all size shape and a variety of colorful cake were its was so attractive we left to catch the bus to go home 11pm shift it was my job entailed so much drama fun and joke I love these residents so much no one could imagine I would sit and watch the strange things that they say I make my rounds and patty those who are unable to help themselves one lady would sit on cry sometimes smile after a while I can understand what is really going through her mind but only god know I question it low and behold out of nowhere I was frightened next to someone creep up on me while cleaning the resident as soon as I turned around I was frightened out of my clothes Barely could imagine seeing this person lord help me it was the lady from room 25 I shout Jesus my heart racing as fast as lighting I could hold my breath I said why are you here she just smile and walk away I get an headache instantly I get the first resident out of the room and back to the activity room to join the others I never drink coffee before and I never take my blood pressure medication I have to tell the other CNA that I will be right I could feel myself getting a bit dizzy I have to hurry across to the nursing and drop myself on the chair it took me 3 minutes to get their I was hot sweating and trying to catch my breath in and out my chest was tight I grasp to get some fresh air I was exhausted Lord my head was bursting I drink some water then relax grab my bag then take my medication within 20 minutes I was up and running again lord o what a fright I told the charge nurse what happen she said god was on your side o yes she was looking flawless her eye brows neatly shave shape like an pear her waist was suck in and her bottom high like blue mountain peak she was beautiful no bump in her face it was smooth like baby bottom she was so attractive her voice is mellow very soft spoken she was very helpful and I was grateful that what we all should be doing caring and sharing with one another I resume my duty picking up the laundry and placing them in the residents rooms complete my all my report and ensure that everyone was accountable for before I clock out have some errands to run I make a few stop just to get some household items and a lights bulk for the oven pay my phone I was taking all precautionary measure

to keep away from Mr. Covid19 I buy
Aloe Vera with a big bottle of honey
one bag full of lemon and rosemary to
make my tea in the morning whenever
I get a chance to do I hop on my bus
and take the long ride I give god thanks
for protecting me always Monday it
was golden as the sun I arise and read
psalm 35 give revenge to the highest
God for sparing my life I heard about
the rising of Mr. Covid19 again he is
very barred face taking more life I
can't wait for him to be arrested or kill
him too bad now lord how long Jesus
patient is of virtues but no mine is
running out I am unable to watch the
destruction upon the land fierce and
furious he continue to roam like
cellular phone boy life several unrest
 score of protesters human outraging
seeking justice but they are in large
crowd the people fail to listen the
hospitals can barely find
accommodation some it may feel like
the world is upon our shoulder right
now but wants us to know that
anything that we are enduring on this
earth now is for a purpose the purpose
may be unknown to us until we asked
god why is he taking us through so
many trials situation and circumstances
it is the key that we must set our hearts
and mind on things that will not
disturb of peace of mind to talk with
god and seek spiritual answer no
problem is too great that our heavenly

father can't fix if we wake up and give him thanks in spite of the current situation remember we are like the chaff that the wind drives away me must see shelter under is covenant in him.

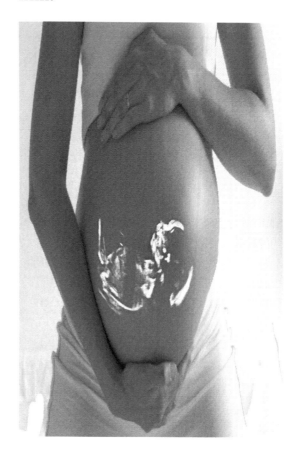

Chapter 21 Positive

I lay my life if it wasn't you Lord than is nothing I will open my mouth and cry aloud to heaven some people have a lot of plan like myself for 2020 but Mr. Covid19 attack the world and turn it upside down what a catastrophe let the

words of my mouth and the meditation
of my heart be acceptable in thy sight o
lord my redeemer lamb of god you will
take away the sins of the world I look at
my life differently today and embrace
the change because it was written the
great depression that I have ever seen
in my age and state of life I understand
the true meaning of thanksgiving life is
short flowing like sand through the
hourglass, running slowly but timely all
to Jesus I surrender Lord all you I
freely give father god the world need a
revival spiritual connection we are in
perilous day I believe in words of the
Almighty god but soon Mr. Covid19
shall become a base in Deuteronomy
4:9 said only take care and keep your
soul diligently lest you forget the things
that your eyes have seen and lest they
depart from your heart all the days of
your life make them know to your
children and your children Moses was
telling the Israelites the word that they
must not change god command and
obey god words this is a clear
indication to what hit the world to it
will spread to all generation of the 4
corners throughout the world lord this
a new transformation of living a
pandemic one will never forget it went
in the same book of Deuteronomy 4.29
but from there you seek the lord your
god and you will find him if you search
after him with all your heart and your
soul it just sad that we have never

spend time with the lord but today family are dedicate to him and invested all the time trying to find god by fasting and praying like a ship without a sail we were drifting in that passage it goes to said when you are in tribulation and all who come upon you in the latter days you will return to the Lord and obey is voice. If my people who call me by my name will not harden their and listen to my voice I will heal the land Moses try to tell the people the law statues and testimonies when they came out of bondage in Egypt but even until this day mankind disobey the ten commandments and choose not to serve God that why is happening on earth if you visit some churches today is not about the gospel anymore it's been a money making entity who remember the story when Jesus went into the temple and the people there were gambling and turn them out and let them know that this is my father house and it's a place of worship they have fun raising every 2 weeks and if you can't contribute to their sometimes your acquitted you from the house of god my god is a jealous god we as Christian need to take a look in our lives and see how we are living Jesus is the light of the world this is a wakeup call God is saying that it's my time until humans begin run for their life we will have more epidemic pandemic and outbreak of multiple disease here and

earth some without remedy people
come we need that turning point in our
live you see god is ready to listen just
talk with him fear not for I am with
you lord comfort the weak and heal the
dying I challenge everyone to make
pray their number priority sacrifice
and pray to God daily let those who
remain shall seek after his kingdom
Lord am but a stranger here am going I
am passing through this barren land
crying screaming mourning suicide
homeless hopeless hungry kidnapping
loathing and shooting the devil need not
to rejoice he will one day be put to
shame lord I look to you this upsurges
is rough like the pacific ocean scary
and frightening experience especially to
the nations.

Chapter 22 The Messiah

Children were dealing with an
unwelcome visitors from out of
nowhere life can only be restored
through Jesus Christ our lord
and Savior who died on Calvary
for you and for me I am ready to
ride out the storm the days are
getting hotter and hotter it just
miserable now but I am coping I
am coping jolly ride in the park
you can see a few children and
their parents trying to play
outside in the still weather the
sun blazing hot I walk across the

playground but away from the small gathering with Mr. Covid19 spiking up I am not applying myself at all the run around and up and down the slides some throwing ball and riding bicycle am glad i enjoy my youth days back in Jamaica I wonder how the kids will ever have a really childhood memories not be able to associated themselves social distant is the remedy now even the birds fly higher these days oh life what a changes back then my cousins would sleep over we cook do our homework together the boys in the family would play with marbles under the big bright moonlight it would look like day our parents and their friends baking the good old Jamaican sweet potato pudding with the slush on top I like mines we didn't have a lot but we got friends and family that allow us to play dance and enjoy ourselves we use the use the Avocado seed to make gig and tree of life to man stick man orange box to make truck bus and car we love to play ring games jump rope and hop scoop summer was nice couldn't wait for school to give holiday in these days kids live their live so different from back

then things and time change its
technology world time they can't
even do arithmetic unless they
are on home school as given me a
wider knowledge base on these
children interaction and
development it funny in a way
that am learning from them lord
help us I observed that they are
so hook on video games more
than ever outside activities no
recreational lifestyle again due to
this pandemic is great for them to
do sports a matter of fact life
depend on free oxygen from
heaven it help the lungs to
function when you inhaling that
fresh air it not easy for the
children I can imagine how it is
with them they must feel
aggressive to not be able to
participate frustration linger in
their minds this life can make
anyone imagination to go wild
we are walking on thin line if
seems like the equator bordering
them for substantiating greatness
in they in this trouble world so
 sad my little has no play mate
now but we stick together the
children are anchor they feel like
they are in chain prison or hold
as hostage in their own homes let
pray for them seek counseling
and get the require help if
necessary to prevent depression

and anxiety stage one day things
will turn around soon god is in
control of this terrible situation
our true selves confident will
enable us to move away from
negative thinking and build the
world confident around this too
shall pass in the book of
Revelation 6:7,8 it talks about the
fourth sealed wide spread death
on earth I hear voice of the
fourth living creature said come
and see so I looked and behold a
pale horse and the name of him
who sat upon it was Death, and
hades followed with him and
power was given to him over
fourth of the earth to kill with
sword with hunger with Death
and by the beast of the earth god
words speak power over the land
we must obey him and turn from
our wicked ways have faith in
him seek refuge in him God is
working on all of behave but we
must asked him for is forgiven of
our sins Easter was the story of
past over when Moses deliver the
Israelites out of bondage the
death demon didn't attack god
children because the blood was
on the true believers in Christ
door so it was pass over in this
time god will protect is chosen
people death is sure in book of
Corinthians it stated also

therefore if anyone is in Christ he has been a new creature the old things as pass away behold the new has come we have to accept where now and where we are coming god has a plan for all of us here on earth life teaches us to love one another according to john 3 verse 16 for god so love the world that he gave is only begotten son that who so ever believe in shall perish but behave everlasting life I believe in the promises that god will come one day again for us and I will live in paradise the angels are standing at the gate of heaven to open and received us unto is kingdom all is children.

Chapter 23 The Word

When the trumpet of the lord
shall sound and the die in Christ
shall arise and meet in the air
judgement day is a must this is
beginning of the new awakening
God will hear our cry and healed
the land massive invasion of Mr.
Covid19 causes millions of death
throughout the world life
continue to fade away just like
the grass that wither and die
 people losing family, friends, and
love ones separation leave home
broken once more today I turn
to the book of David one of the

greatest apostle Paul as spoken
before now this psalm 27 The
Lord is my light and my salvation
whom shall I fear then my head
shall exalt my enemies o gracious
father I stand before you
almighty god to conquer the
enemies which is Lord build a
fence around us shine your light
before us lead us lord my people
cry out to god thank you Jesus
for your grace will you anchor
hold and grip the solid rock Jesus
is the rock in a weary land my
God o great thou hart you are
our tower of strength father I
give myself completely to you god
we have forgotten about you lord
and only you can restored life I
pray that you will fight the enemy
of death no physician on earth is
greater than you lord o Jesus you
will do it again lord to you I give
all the praise fill me up lord o
lord I need thee touch our life in
a special way I pray dear lord
that the universe is calling to you
 bind us together lord for all the
world to see that the time has
come for us to love and care lord
I can do all thing through you
who strengthens me show mercies
lord show us mercies I prayed
Amen money have no true
meaning now to those who
bragger and boast about it

material things become is like
nothing during this time only the
fit of the fit will survived the
bible said o beyond to them with
children Mr. Covid19 come to
show us that we must look to you
love and recognize you as lord
and Savior Lord let the world
bow down before your throne
and draw closer to you lord am
longing for home my heavenly
home where there will be no
sicken are sadden there I stand
 upon the mountain looking down
in the valley o what a joy this
would when we all get to heaven
I can just imagine the beauty that
await us we can't understand the
misery surrounding Mr. Covid19
only god can he must die one day
and peace returned to the
universe my deepest condolences
go out to those who have lost
their family friends parents
grandparents children
grandchildren nieces nephews
cousins and love one to people
over the entire world that is
battling with the pandemic stay
strong and never let go of God's
unchanging hands my peace I
leave with you my peace I give
unto and to you for all of us who
remain remember that there is
hope in king Jesus their hope in
god we are not failure and we are

not walking by sight but by faith
is the substance of all things pass
and all things present and things
to come keep safe trust and obey
your master calling if your
thirsty and weary come run for
your life the song said just as I
am without one plea that god has
shed his blood for me come to
him if you heavy laden.

Chapter 24 Accepting Christ

Come earnestly tenderly Jesus is
calling for sinner to come home
just come render your heart and

not your garment come Jesus
need you stay focus and live by is
promises come he said when you
go through the waters I will be
with you god voice is gracious in
thunder I can't even imagine is
greatness of is power i am
 continue work in this volatile
conditions testing continue every
14 days to ensure that all staff
remain negative I know that man
on earth is prefect but I try to
take all the precautionary
measure for me and my daughter
to stay for me and my household
we served the lord we don't have
visitors but we travel out is only
the both of us I make sure that
when I get the chance to call back
home I encourage my 4 other
children and my parents to stay
home a lot of nursing home
assistant care giver are doing the
same without a job in this
American you cannot function
but I honor your lord you keep
safe and I stand in the liberty of
you lord great is thy faithfulness
God you're an awesome God he
will never leave us or forsake us
love yourself but each and
everyone in the world of all colors
culture form able and disabled
nationally and race in your
prayer lord keep them safe stay
home can save life my voyage

continue I am steadfast facing
desolation lack of interaction
sometime I feel dismay but not
drowning as a child of god my
father order his angels to guard
me all the ways I have no need to
panic because god will be here
with us he will keep us safe and
sound Lord I trust you the clock
is ticking the time is going we are
almost in July time wait on no
one I write to book to encourage
someone that god care no matter
the situation he still care believe I
was their losing a child nowhere
to live I was in a state in the USA
no family support I cry out with
only 2 days to live the apartment
he make a way when even this I
can't understand what happen
but he come through for me am
a living testimony I share my
story with the world to let you all
know that Mr. Covid19 is not
great obstacles and don't be
afraid strongly believe that my
book will touch life in a special
way God is good all the time I
look at the animals they life and
God provide for them he
speaking above the raven and say
don't worry about tomorrow
because it provide for itself that
so true life is like an orbit that
revolves around the earth
spinning. Constantly but only one

man control it and that is Jesus Christ who is the head of our life so my dear beloved children stay home stay safe stay positive stay strong there is no comparison when it come to your health adjustments can be uncomfortable but get with the flow I love and miss you guys read the bible to gain greater insight of what god have to reveal to mankind on earth kindle with him more than always am hanging up now my phone is beeping my battery is running am clock in on the 11pm shift am out by now if I don't see you all again I will meet you over on the other at pearly white gate we sing unto the lord a new song and dance to melodious praise and worship song there be no more crying there thank you Jesus I leave this with you all be on your guard stand firm in the faith be courageous be strong 1 Corinthians 16:13 I live an extraordinary one that make you I am today evaluating myself to pursue my goals my children are my inspiration to watch them grow and been their education and with the direction of spiritual guidance.

Chapter 25 Great Sense Humor

I develop a true sense of who I really
am, a child of God I never
underestimate the power that he have
in high places I used to doubt a lot of
things that happen around my
characteristics lead to proceed great
vision and they become reality
whenever I dream it will play out that
why am not marvel about time great
depression I know that god that Christ
live inside of me no matter my downfall
i get brush myself of and start over
again it's a crazy world out their but
you definitely has to stay conscious.
This is a new day gosh, it Monday am
off am going to do my morning

devotion and go right back to bed I am
extremely tired so exhausted too doing
a few double at work it just burn me
out my feet feel soar I have to put them
to soak in some Epsom salt with
lukewarm water anytime I get no much
to do since I wash over night iron pack
away the clothes in my closet I am tired
my eyes are red blood turn the
television on the next thing I know is
that my eyes are heavy I lay down
because wanted to sleep o life I feel like
I was sun drowning even though I
wasn't getting enough rest I launch my
body out wrapped up in my blanket
and sleep it was 4:15 pm it was a bit
cooler inside than I expected to be I
pull my blanket up over my head I look
across to see if my little was their she
curl up in the corner fast asleep when
open the door on the patio it was
raining with gusty winds trees swinging
from left to right crashing limb falling
to ground I watch for a while then went
by inside set my water and do my feet I
was so hungry toast bread I make 2
sandwiches turkey breast lettuce
tomato slices I lovely glass of orange
juice my appetite freely squeeze with
my hands no sugar added notice were
on the I taste good please remember
that tomorrow to check the mailbox
this girl is something else the rain
continue to lashed outside the trees are
crying lord have mercy I wake up nagi
let she cool off next was her bathroom

time she wash her face brush her teeth and comb her hair she said is it raining I yes let it rain we need the water it was too hot and humid the tree were drying the road dusty she and we play a game of dominoes read story and check my email to see if my job send me something no significant was there that I close we watch a movie while she do her school work funny enough she is always quite no one hardly know if someone lived at 925 you never know I the struggle continue its a lovely for dinner we have some left over chicken I boil potatoes steam veggie I enjoyed it so much yeah she lick her finger and mom I enjoy my dinner I went to my room she wash the dishes clean the stove and came back to the I ate an orange too it was for a long time have eat some so delicious and with arrangement of the colorful veggie is was very attractive to my eyes no one talk about Mr. Covid19 that much I stop watching the news in general I was too and tired of hearing about it we call back home and London my sibling was safe and some everyone was happy to hear that we are all doing well my nephew turns 12 years old o boy time fly he is very tall now lovely smile he is so handsome I miss London it was my home ground, life good then we ride the Bakerloo Line from Brixton to Wood Green and 7 Sister ,Croydon and all over East and West London I was 25 years old at the time Tony Blair was the Prime Minister at the time west beautiful sightseeing Buckingham Palace, the great shopping I touch base just checking to see how they all are doing business throughout the world is struggling to survive the pandemic so do the life of everyone it just heartrending to see the facial expression on people face this longing to come to terms of the killer Mr. Covid19 I can only advise them to pray the news is headache I stay away from the network I love scrabble but I can't manage puzzle the piece time too much time to put it together am fascinating by Tom & Jerry cartoon or The Simpson sometimes the Jefferson I just get my laughter and giggle hard I love old Thomas I am use by him my oldest brother turn 50 2 weeks ago but stay home and celebrate no cook out just relax with wife and 3 children that sucks hush brother continue give thanks for life you complete a half a century big man no as people live there life going about their business things has gotten worst now more than ever death and more death it's no surprise to me base on what Doctor Fauci was told the nation it become a dangerous outbreak in south Florida rising case every single day I go D & Q and buy 2 medium size sundaes I am humbling myself in the sight of glory the erosion of this pandemic is wearing down the

world is human disaster the more we
maintain our distant wear protect
grease and stay at home follow your
heart listen to your instinct do good the
flag will flow hero will die healthcare
risk our life we are trying to work hard
on the ground we are the most
vulnerable and essential work we face
the daily task to save life and we are at
risk to ourselves family and love one
but through it all I learn to trust in god
and live my mind is set on Jesus he can
make the impossible become possible
this pandemic change everything here
on earth dramatically a word to the
wise one seek spiritual knowledge and
draw closer to god who is our soon
coming king press on with faith stand
brave god also said it finish I am the
Alpha and the omega the beginning and
the end to all who are thirsty I will give
freely from the spring of the water of
life Revelation 21:6 let all the earth fear
the lord let all the inhabitants stand in
awe of him for he spoke and it was
done he command and it stood fast
psalms 33:8,9 you can assured that god
is in control of Covid19
Sleep in the morning to heal the broken
as I continue to pray. The mere fact is
my beloved, our God is prepared and
can't get over the screams, tears rolling
down the face of families grieving,
unable to hug each other as the wave of
deaths sweep through the world.

During this time lives change
dramatically, despite the
outbreak rent increase, inflation rises,
high food prices escalate, the climate
gets worse, global warming becomes
another issue, this is really
unbelievable. Despite the rampage of
the deadly disease the heart of men
continues to get wicked no cure for
mental wickedness. Hardships grow
dreadful on the Treasure Coast
children getting sick day by day
hospitals overcrowded Doctors, Nurses,
shortage continues omg I am truly lost
for words, boldly behind this fearful
attack we continue to work assiduously
dedicating myself to the only life that I
now know lockdown.

Made in the USA
Columbia, SC
27 February 2023

12989895R00054